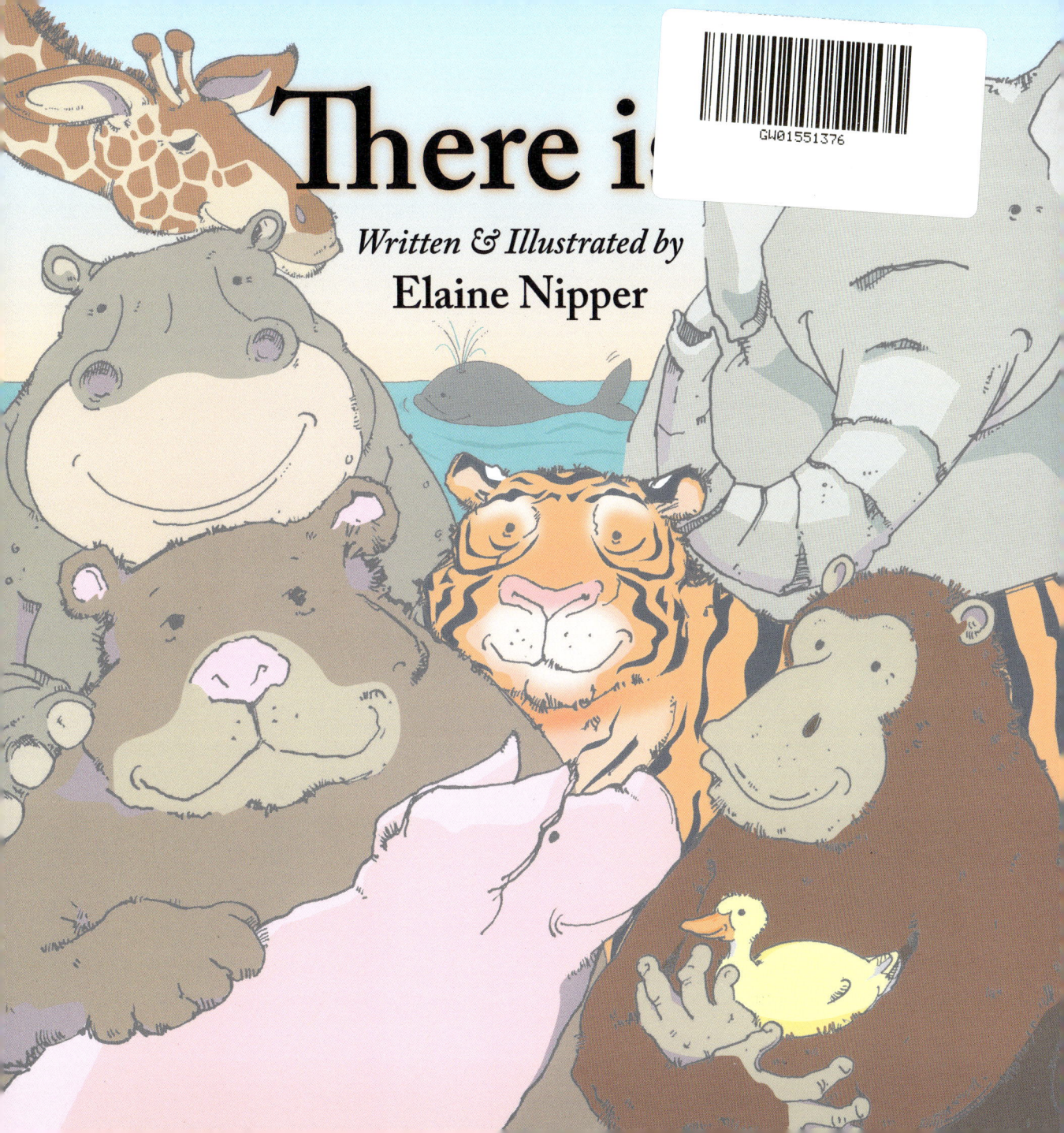

...a bear on my chair.

He doesn't care!

...a whale in our bath.

That made us laugh!

...a hippo in my bed.

Who answers to Fred!

...a duck in the soup.

I hope she doesn't poop!

...a monkey on my bike.

Taking us on a hike!

...a giraffe in the park.

...a tiger on the bus.

What a lot of fuss!

...a pig on
the swing.

Having a fling!

...an elephant on the slide.

Who's a little bit wide!

Or is there?